The Managers' Guide to Getting Control Of Your Business

The Managers' Guide to Getting Control Of Your Business

A Series of "How-to, Hands-on" Procedures for Effectively Handling Management Issues

Mel Lofurno

iUniverse, Inc.
New York Lincoln Shanghai

The Managers' Guide to Getting Control Of Your Business
A Series of "How-to, Hands-on" Procedures for Effectively Handling Management Issues

iUniverse, Inc.

For information address:
iUniverse, Inc.
2021 Pine Lake Road, Suite 100
Lincoln, NE 68512
www.iuniverse.com

ISBN: 0-595-31568-2 (pbk)
ISBN: 0-595-66338-9 (cloth)

Printed in the United States of America

Contents

Introduction

WHY READ THIS BOOK?

This book is about change; specifically, making changes to improve your business. It is a guide for those responsible for the financial health of a business. In other words, this book is *for Managers*. I have written this guide in a simple, straightforward manner, addressing the use of the basic building blocks of a business. My rational for making it basic is that if you are refining a process, you must start by evaluating the underlying reasons for having the process to start or if you are creating a new business, you must define the desired results before starting.

This book is intended for use as a guide for making changes in the running of an on-going business or for establishing the operating systems of a new business.

If you are not satisfied with something in your business…if you think some part of it could be better…if the business is running you…if you are not having fun (by the way, my definition of "fun" is successfully meeting a challenge)…reading this book is a start to making the change happen. However, if you only read without doing the follow-through actions at the end of each Session, all you will accomplish is to have provided a few hours of diversion.

If you are just establishing you business, I suggest you read the entire book and then prioritize the order in which you address implementation of the systems.

This book is also about balance. Every situation offers the opportunity for action or inaction; use the extremes judiciously. I encourage managers to identify the extremes and to operate within the mid 40% range. Most people value consistency. It provides a level of stability and helps to avoid surprises. I realize I am describing an intangible concept and offer this example to clarify the concept. If you visualize complete chaos as one extreme and complete bureaucracy as the other, you realize that neither will promote successful business. Determine the procedures you need to carry out your strategies and implement those. Strive to operate somewhere in the mid-range. To accomplish this you must first be aware of the overall situation and second you must use judgment in execution.

Our actions have consequences; intended and un-intended. Nothing happens in a vacuum…and there are no secrets. Strive to make the best judgments based on the information available to you at the time. These Sessions are designed to help you grow in that endeavor.

And this book is about honor, the bedrock on which you manage and about discipline, accountability and respect…for yourself and others. Don't expect to manage others if you cannot manage yourself.

But mostly this book is about leadership…positioning yourself as the leader of your business in the minds of those on whom you rely. Managers accomplish things through the efforts of others. Those on whom you depend to get things done must believe in you; trust that you know where you are taking the business and how you will get there. Your quest is to manage through goal-driven, proactive, principle-centered leadership…and you must work at this in all aspects of your behavior.

A colleague once said to me, "You've got to know what to do when you don't know what to do." My goal in writing this book, is to provide a "business compass" that managers can use to guide them through events.

I envision this book to be used as a tune-up manual for business because, just as you tune-up your car, portfolio or anything else for optimum performance, you must occasionally check and adjust your business to meet your goals.

Time and energy are two of your most valuable resources…both are limited. In order to make the most of each available for the growth and protection of your business, you must have procedures in place to handle the routine matters of business. This book provides a guide for tuning-up your business to accomplish that. If you are just starting out, it provides a "to-do" list of systems and procedures you should put into place.

One more thing about change…It's going to occur. You can either sit back, watch it happen and react, or you can manage proactively and help shape the changes. Just be sure to recognize those things within your control and those over which you have little or no influence and act accordingly.

The important thing is for you to act. Do the actions suggested at the end of each Session. These will help you stay grounded in your goals. This "guide" will provide specific actions for you to take to achieve the results you seek. Becoming proficient at managing is similar to learning how to master other challenging endeavors; it requires practice.

It's not necessary to read this cover-to-cover. Use this as a reference handbook and read those topics as you have the need or interest or open the book at random and read the topic…and carry out the action steps. The benefits to you and your business will result only from *your* application of the principles.

Use this book as a "Tune-up Manual" for your business. Consider your management systems as the "engine" of your business. Just as you occasionally "tune-up" the engine of your car, you should examine your management systems to ensure they are giving you the output you want. Much of this book is devoted to your thinking process…you must know where you are taking your business and what results you want from it. Just as engine tuners adjust for specific applications, you must adjust your systems and procedures to deliver the application of your policies. For example, engine tuners will use different settings to tune for horsepower or fuel economy. Engine tuners have three primary elements with which to work—air, fuel and ignition. You have your **vision, strategies and execution.**

AUTHOR'S CREDENTIALS

Danish physicist Niels Bohr said, "An expert is a person who has made all the mistakes that can be made in a very narrow field." I haven't made ALL the mistakes yet and I learned long ago to avoid those who present themselves as "experts." What I offer in this book is a compilation of practical ways to apply the business management principles I have learned (so far) over my thirty-nine year career. I gleaned this knowledge from colleagues and mentors at Dupont and the German chemical company, Degussa, as well as from our many world-class customers and competitors. Since 2000, I have demonstrated that the principles I formerly applied around the world in the electronics industries, are also applicable to a wide range of businesses. The principles are constant; the implementation is adjusted as appropriate for the culture of the industry.

The Sessions of this book were adapted from a series of monthly articles that first appeared in *Compoundings*, the trade publication of the Independent Lubricant Manufacturers Association.

Session 1
The Basic Elements of Managing

Management Style

As a business manager, you know first-hand the results of "the impartiality of the market." At some time, business will be affected by market events over which you have no control. By identifying those situations and conditions you can control, and taking appropriate preparatory action; you will be better positioned to respond. The objective is to manage pro-actively rather than reactively; to manage in such a way as to prevent problems from arising, instead of solving problems after they occur. Take time to develop your policies, systems and procedures. You cannot prevent every problem, but controlling those you can, you will have more time to handle the un-expected.

Managing in this pro-active, principle-centered style of management will instill confidence in those on whom you depend…your employees, customers, suppliers and bankers, to list a few. It isn't complicated, but it requires discipline. Business operates in a continuum, no event occurs in a vacuum. Every action and every failure to act, has consequences—some intended, some unintended. Your responsibility as the manager is to identify opportunities and threats and act accordingly.

Sir Ernest Shackleton, the Antarctic explorer, wrote in his log, "Loneliness is the penalty of leadership, but the man who has to make the decisions is assisted greatly if he feels that there is no uncertainty in the minds of those who follow him, and that his orders will be carried out confidently and in expectation of success."

The key is instilling confidence in those we lead. Leaders accomplish this through the way they behave—how they manage their time and what they accomplish. In other words, "how you get the right things done."

Getting Things Done

Consider these four questions;

- "What's on your mind?"
- "Where do you want to be in three years?"
- "Are you on track?"
- "Where are you now?"

A typical response to the first question is, "How can I get more things done?"

The answer is "Through people." To make this happen, they must accept you as their leader. They must have confidence in your leadership ability and believe that you know where you want to take the business and how you will do it. Prioritizing and focusing demonstrates the clarity of purpose needed to gain their support.

Being able to answer the next three questions in crystal-clear words is one of the first steps to being recognized as a leader. This requires having developed a plan, implementing it, consistently measuring results and making adjustments.

Pro-active management through leadership has three fundamental components:

1. Development of the plan
2. Getting the right people
3. Execution of the plan

Development of the Plan

The strategic plan defines the desired future state, documents the current state and provides the roadmap for achieving the goal. It is treated as a living document and is actively used as a guide in managing the business. Key issues that must be addressed in order to achieve the goal are identified and strategies, tactics and action items clearly defined.

Getting the Right People

People are the greatest asset of your business. You will achieve your goals through them. Your must find motivated people and give them an environment in which they can succeed…set the direction and provide the resources. You must delegate, measure against defined milestones and hold people accountable.

Execution of the Plan

There are many ideas and wishes. Leaders make them happen. Most failures are the result of failure to execute the plan. You must set timelines and provide feedback as the key actions in the execution.

Through purposeful, focused efforts in planning, leading and managing, you will promote trust in your leadership and increase the probability of effectively responding to market forces and achieving your business goals.

Action Items:

Write on a piece of paper your responses to the four questions posed under **"Getting Things Done"** and put it in the back of this book. Your responses to each question may be as little as one word but no more than three sentences. If you need more than that to express your answers, you don't really know the answers. Re-write until you make your points in crystal-clear language.

Have these Action Items completed before moving on to another Session. Let's establish a practice right now by setting completion dates—for yourself and for others—and hold accountable.

Session 2
A Structure for Managing

What is Your Goal?

Session 1 outlined the initial steps in establishing you as a competent leader in the minds of your employees and others on whom the success of your business depends. The objective is to identify those actions that people associate with leaders. You as the business manager want to behave in ways that will earn the confidence of others by demonstrating your ability to know where you are taking the business and how you will do it.

Getting Things Done

Most people who accomplish the "right things" at the "right time" usually have a plan in place, have prioritized the issues and focused on them in an organized fashion. In other words, they had a plan.

We listed the basic elements for establishing your program as:

- Development of your plan
- Bringing the "right" people on board
- Execution of your plan

This Session addressed those basic elements that are needed for a "workable" plan. These are simple thoughts and the discipline of writing them clearly and concisely is a good start for being able to demonstrate that you have a vision for your business and "see" the way to achieve it.

The Plan

The critical aspects of a plan are clarity and feasibility. Write the plan so those who help execute it have a crystal-clear understanding and a strong belief in the probability of success.

Start with an outline in developing the plan. It will be a "living" document—you will review it on a frequent, regular timeline and adjust as necessary.

The first step is to define your goal; what you want the end result to be. State your business *VISION* or *GOAL* in simple, direct terms identifying measurable results. My target is to be able to state the vision, in about three sentences.

Next, define the *MISSION* in clear statements. This states what you must accomplish in order to achieve your goal. Try to say this in about three sentences also.

What are those things that you must overcome in order to achieve your mission? These are the *KEY ISSUES* you face...potential "show-stoppers." Identify the top five or six to keep the plan manageable; as items are completed, you will add additional.

Now list some *STRATEGIES* you will employ to address the key issues. You will typically develop one to three for each key issue.

Strategies will remain merely ideas until you identify the *TACTICS* you will use to carry them out. This is the time to commit your *TIMELINE* to paper. Identify who is accountable for what and by when. This timeline is one of your management tools for tracking progress against goals. Those accountable for completion of the tactics must work with those who will carry out the *ACTION ITEMS* and *TASKS* to ensure they understand what is required and they have the tools, resources and support necessary for completion.

The other elements of your strategic business plan will provide details and analysis of the total business. Start by writing what you know; add details as you acquire them. Set a timeline for gathering bits of information. Step-by-step your plan will come together.

The Business

The Industry

Your Company

Your Products

Pricing

Positioning

The Market

Customers

Market Size & Trends

Competition (In-kind/Not-in-kind)

Suppliers

Advertising

Target market segments

Market Share

Sales Projections

Marketing, Sales & Distribution

Sales Force

Target customers

Financials

Statement of Cash flow

Balance sheet

Income statement

Pro Forma overview

Risks

Management Structure/Team

Senior/key management   Operating management

Advisory board   Contracted Services

Start now to formalize your plan. If you already have one, review and up-date it. Don't use the excuse of waiting until you have all the information. Start documenting what you know now and add details as you acquire them. The plan will serve several purposes at this point; it will force you to think through your goals, give you a road-map for reaching them and demonstrate to others that you are managing and leading your business.

Action Items:

Write your vision for your business. If you've already done this, review it for validity now. Revise as needed. Try to do this in four sentences or less.

Do the same for your business mission.

Review the key issues that can prevent you from realizing carrying out your mission. Re-state them as needed. Remember, if you have more than six; re-word to get to the appropriate level of the issues.

Session 3
Setting Expectations and Measuring Results

Who Does What…and by When?

Sessions 1 & 2 addressed the overall importance of management style in accomplishing things through leading people in the execution of a plan. Session 2 focused on the elements of "The Plan." Now, you have your plan and must implement it. If we think of your plan as the "vehicle"; the "engine" that propels it to your goal is **people**. You, as the leader, are the "driver" and must provide the direction and support, measure the progress and provide feedback to those doing the job.

Building Your Team

Successful business managers achieve results through the efforts of people. The first principle is to have the "right" people in the key positions. As part of your plan, you developed an organizational structure for your business, now you will find qualified, enthusiastic people for those positions. My experience teaches this is a challenging process and I know of no easy or sure-fire way to do it, but with discipline and judgment on your part, the probability of success is increased. A step-wise approach will help you in prioritizing and focusing on the task at hand.

- Develop position descriptions or job instructions for each position in your organizational chart

- Critically evaluate your current employees against the qualifications required for each position

- For each position, interview qualified current employees and other candidates identified from a search

- Make your selection using your judgment considering skill-sets, motivation, experience and "fit" with others in your team

The manner in which you conduct this part of your management tasks will have a very strong impact on how your team views your leadership skills. This will be time-consuming but do not rush. This is one management responsibility where it will take longer to correct a mistake than to get it right the first time. Be diligent in your approach and expeditious in your moves. Consider using professional Human Resource services for initial screening, but the final decision is yours.

The Direction

Now that your team is in place, you must provide the direction in which you want them to help you take the business. Conduct a group meeting in which you share the main points of your business plan. This way all will hear the same words. Use this occasion to build "team spirit." Emphasize to all that they are part of a sophisticated team in that each relies on the other to meet commitments—such as arriving for meetings prepared and on time, submitting reports complete and on time and completing assignments on schedule. Then meet individually and ensure that these points are crystal-clear in the minds of each:

- Your expectations of their performance

- Agreement on the goals for which each will be held accountable

- Your understanding of their concerns and expectations

- The "mile-stones" by which you will measure their performance

- How and when you will provide feedback

- Your commitment to providing resources necessary for them to do their job

The Follow-through

This is the management effort that translates all the foregoing work into results...and the area that distinguishes "leaders" from managers who merely go through the paces. Here again the discipline of prioritizing, focusing, measuring and adjusting increase the probability of success.

- Meet with your employees on a scheduled basis

- Review accomplishments against goals

- Analyze reasons for any action items missing completion dates

- Re-establish completion dates

- Adjust resources as necessary

Put high value on this. Without the follow-through effort, it is easier for people to fall into the reactive mode instead of focusing on the action items to drive the project to completion.

In Session 4, we'll look at proven techniques of successful execution.

Action Items:

Review your org chart. If you don't have one, create it.
Write down the primary roles and responsibilities for each position.

Session 4
Execution of the Plan

Making it Happen

In Sessions 1 through 3, we have outlined the development of your business plan and key procedures for building your team. Now that you have your plan and the people to carry it out, we are at the point where "the rubber meets the road"—putting the plan into action. Until you do this, your plan remains an idea—a dream—a wish—a hope. It's your job to make it become reality. This is where you will be challenged to maintain your self-discipline of management. You will experience situations in which you will be tempted to operate in the reactive mode, but through diligently focusing on the action items developed in your plan, and properly leading your people, you can proactively accomplish the mission.

Hope is Not a Method—Gordon R. Sullivan & Michael V. Harper

I have chosen the title of the book by Sullivan and Harper (Random House 1996) as the heading of this section because it cryptically describes the challenge facing business managers…and I recommend reading the book.

How do you convert the plan into reality? *Hope is not a method*—you must act; and before acting, you must plan.

Define the path-forward, establish responsibilities for action items and follow up. Lead the team in taking action to accomplish the tasks. Do this by clearly stating the objective and diligently and consistently measuring the progress. The first step in implementing the plan is to ensure that your people understand what they must do and when it must be accomplished. You must tell them, make sure they have the necessary resources, measure their progress and adjust as necessary.

The Gantt Chart is a commonly used tool for managing individual and group progress in carrying out the action steps. It is a graphic timeline that helps keep the work and expectations in perspective. The chart may be anything from a simple table drawn on graph paper (example below) to those generated by software packages, but the important features are the steps to be completed in order to accomplish the objective, the starting and completion dates and the person accountable. Typically, you will have an overall chart tracking the major actions and individual charts for each person with detailed milestones.

<u>Simple Gantt Chart</u>

Program Name											
	Time Period										Person
Action	1	2	3	4	5	6	7	8	9	10	Accountable
Action or Milestone 1											Name 1
Action or Milestone 2											Name 2
Action or Milestone 3											Name 3
Action or Milestone 4											Name 4

The Process

It is an effective management technique to develop the actions/milestones jointly with your team. Later, as the team gains experience, you will be able to define the goals and they will prepare their individual Gantt Charts as a tool for managing the parts of the program for which they are accountable. Depending on the scope of the program, you may have a one-page chart or many pages. Strive for a reasonable balance in the actions/milestones. Don't break out trivial tasks; on the other hand, don't broad-brush to the extent that the significance is lost. With experience you will find the proper balance. The more reasonable this is, the easier it will be for people to buy into the program and take ownership.

Schedule regular meetings to review progress against the timeline. Focus on those items that are behind schedule. Determine the reason, arrange for resources as needed and adjust the timeline appropriately. Review items that are completed or ahead of schedule, shift resources to other items and adjust appropriately. Don't waste peoples' time discussing items that are on schedule. Maintain your focus. The manner in which you follow-through in monitoring the progress of those doing the work will be your mark as a leader in the minds of others.

Action Items:

Develop and use a Gantt chart for your next meeting...then use it for follow-up at the following meeting. Make it a routine management tool.

Session 5
Leading Effective Meetings

The Messages We Send

How do we go about "managing through leadership"? The simple answer is, "by instilling in others the belief that we know what is to be accomplished and how to get it done." But how do we instill this belief? Since most people form beliefs based on their observation of behavior, it makes sense that we should behave in ways to promote this perception. The primary issue is that we must act out of sincerity. We must believe in the goal and the actions we take should clearly support achieving those goals...our actions must reflect our words. Not only in the "grand" things we do, but also in the daily routine. Stay aware of how you spend your time; and equally important, of how you ask your people to spend theirs. In earlier columns, I addressed measuring peoples' results against goals. Your responsibility is to support them in succeeding; do not create unnecessary tasks for them.

Another Meeting?

Meetings are one of the most visible management activities...and they are often viewed more negatively than positively. As a leader, think about how your use of meetings impacts the perception of your management ability and your commitment to effective use of time. When should you call a meeting? Simple answer, only when necessary. This is an opportunity to demonstrate effective leadership.

Before scheduling a meeting, you must be crystal-clear in defining:

- The purpose of the meeting
- The desired results

Then ask yourself:

- Who must participate?
- When is the most effective time?
- How much time will be needed?
- Where is the most efficient place?

The Mechanics of Meetings

In deciding if a meeting is needed, first define the objective. Ideally, meetings will be a tool through which the decision-makers evaluate information and arrive at the desired path-forward. Avoid the temptation to call a meeting for the purpose of passing along information. You can accomplish this more economically without calling a meeting. Get the necessary background information—and the agenda—in the hands of the participants in advance…allow enough time for them to digest it and gather other data as needed….then meet to make decisions. Naturally, there will be exceptions; the sensitivity of the topic or in timing, may justify holding a meeting to pass along certain information.

Who should participate? Again, a simple answer, only those who can contribute. This includes the decision-makers and, if needed, "experts" to provide details on the background data. Normally, there is no need for the experts to sit in for the whole meeting; if you follow your agenda; they can arrive as needed at specific times. Others in your organization, who will be affected by the decisions made, should be notified in a timely fashion.

At the start of the meeting,—(note: effective leaders start meetings on time)—review the purpose, the desired results and your proposed agenda. It's a good technique to have these statements as a slide or written on a "flip-chart." Solicit "up-grades" from the participants and when you have buy-in, follow the agenda. Arrange to have someone record cryptic notes on "flip-charts" to help keep the group focused. Keep these visible during the meeting and use them to write the meeting notes at the conclusion. Also, designate someone to serve as "meeting guide" to help keep the discussion focused on the topic at hand.

Keep the meeting on track, clearly define accountability and timing for action items and adjourn on time. Issue the meeting notes soon, the next day is a good target.

Meetings are costly, but through good meeting design and execution, you can maximize the benefits. The leader has the responsibility to ensure that attendance in the meeting is the best use of each participant's time. Demonstrate through your meeting etiquette that you value their time—lead productive meetings.

Action Items:

Send out an agenda a week before your next meeting. Give participants and opportunity to get other issues on the table at the start of the meeting.
Critically evaluate if you invited some who did not need to spend time there…could they have been informed as necessary later?

Session 6
Where to Spend your Time

Effective Management—The Balance between Chaos and Bureaucracy

"Balanced Management", like many other necessities for survival is first noticed through its absence. Achieving a "balance" in the way they manage their business is an on-going goal of effective managers. They stay "tuned-in" to what their employees are feeling. A sense of balance in the managers' style conveys reasonableness, competence and control. Employees will be the first to notice an imbalance. This is a critical aspect of instilling confidence in the leadership and management skills.

We've all experienced the frustration of dealing with organizations paralyzed by bureaucratic procedures...and the frustration of dealing with those who operate haphazardly. Both are energy-wasting and counter-productive. So, how do you find the balance in your organization? You must develop and exercise good business judgment. Let's say you're not one of the lucky few born with "good judgment." The only option is to develop through practice. Be aware of your mode of behavior and work to become more effective.

Consider the observation that goes;

"We must find people with good judgment."

"Right! How does one get good judgment?"

"From experience"

"Right! How does one get experience?"

"From poor judgment"

Think about this. We talk about the need for planning, but plans without actions remain only dreams. Find the balance between your efforts in planning and your actions in carrying out the plan. You can only gain this insight through experience. Managers need to develop plans and execute them judiciously based on the best information available. With each effort, your experience grows, so don't postpone opportunities to upgrade your ability to make good decisions and to improve the probability of success. Learn from your experiences, and give your employees the opportunity to do the same.

The most critical area that managers must address is the proper balance of involvement somewhere between "the big picture" and "the details." The optimal point is not fixed, but varies depending on the situation. Work to consistently achieve the "proper" level of involvement. One helpful management tool for doing this is to be aware of your efforts. How do you balance your time among the planning, leading and managing responsibilities?

Modes of Management—Planning/Leading/ Managing

As a manager, you are operating in one of these modes at any given time. Depending on your management level, you will spend a higher percentage of time in one of these modes than the others overall, but you will continually be moving among them in managing your business. Track your time for a few days during the month and evaluate your balance. This table shows the guidelines I suggest. Look at this over a month—short term you may focus on a particular area due to deadlines, emergencies and other outside factors.

Guidelines—Managers' Efforts			
Management Level	Planning	Leading	Managing
Senior	70%	25%	5%
Middle	25%	50%	25%
First-line	10%	20%	70%

Senior management and owners set the direction and provide the resources to the organization. Middle managers implement and oversee programs leading to the goal. First-line managers carry out the actions. All accomplish their responsibilities through the efforts of others. Balancing the management mode to your level demonstrates managerial maturity and instills in others confidence in your "leadership."

Policies, Systems and Procedures

To help establish and maintain the proper balance between "doing paperwork" and "doing work", it is necessary to determine what information is needed to run the business efficiently. Procedures provide consistent responses to similar events and ways to capture routine information but without analysis and review they may be a waste of time. Unnecessary procedures are counterproductive and your employees know that. To avoid this situation, first develop the policies by which you will operate your business, then design the systems to support the policies and then implement the procedures for employees to carry out the policies. Review procedures on a regular basis and eliminate those that are no longer useful.

Action Items:

Keep a written log to track where you spend your time for a week. Evaluate if you are making the greatest contribution of your efforts. You want to focus on those jobs that only you can do; let others take care of jobs they can do.

Session 7
Managing Information

Implementing the Principles

"Buy low; sell high." Who argues with <u>that</u> principle as a way of making money? But what exactly must we do in order to consistently do that? Granted, intuition and luck play important roles, and we don't discount these, but a well-developed plan and disciplined execution provide a greater probability of success. The same thing goes for managing your business. *"Act decisively."* Easy to say and recognized as an effective management principle of business leaders, but how do we know what to decide? We are continually making decisions based on the best information available at the time. How do we handle the information on which we base our decisions?

The first step in any undertaking is to gather pertinent information...not only facts, but perceptions and other nuances that may influence the facts. At the outset, there's typically too much, rather than too little information. This may be complicated by the fact that during the fact-gathering stage the line between pertinent and extraneous is often blurred. The following process is a guideline for collecting, using and managing the information relating to a particular goal or objective. This approach is an effective management tool for processing information in a disciplined manner.

Information Handling—Process Diagram

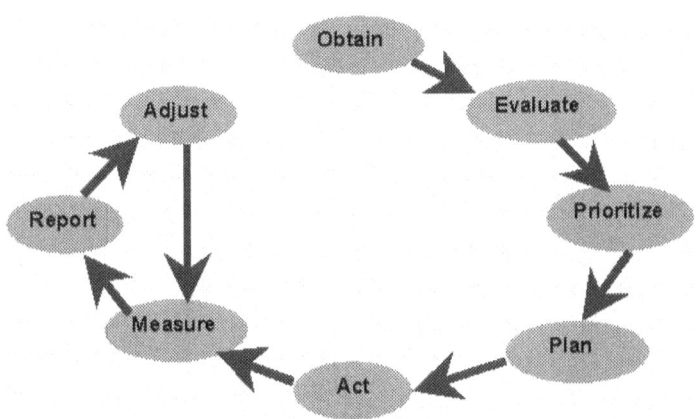

Pulling it All Together and Getting Started

Consider this as an opportunity to test the principles presented in previous Sessions. Identify some area in your business environment that you want to change and apply the process guidelines presented in Sessions 1–6.

Start by defining your:

1)   Objective   (Vision/goal—Session 2)

2)   Timeline and milestones   (Gantt chart—Session 4)

3)   Resources   (Your team—Session 3)

4)   Responsibilities   (Follow-through—Session 3)

Then,

5)   Pulling your team together   (Meeting guidelines—Session 5)

In addition to applying the execution techniques, discipline yourself to be aware of those areas where you spend your time and also the balance between planning and acting. Measure where you spend your time and the results you achieve. Acting without adequate planning produces chaos and few results; planning without focused actions produces "nothing."

The first four steps in the "Process Diagram" are the "preparation phases"; followed by the "action phases." With experience, you will naturally find the balance between "not enough" and "too much" in carrying out each phase. Remember, this is a tool; it is the means through which you accomplish an objective; don't get so caught up in "doing" the process that you lose sight of the accomplishing the objective. Adapt the process to meet the specific needs of your business.

Execution Tips

In the "Obtain" phase, it is better to err on the side of collecting too much data. During the "Evaluation" phase you can eliminate that which is non-meaningful. After arranging the information in manageable categories; analyze for results versus effort and prioritize the action steps needed to achieve the objective. Focus your resources according to your prioritization and develop the plan for accomplishing them.

Acting on the plan is the first phase of the "action" steps. Record and measure the results of the actions; report and analyze the results and adjust as needed. At this point you will go into a refinement loop of measuring, reporting and adjusting until you have optimized the effort. Be reasonable and recognize when you have reached the point of diminishing returns.

You can use this process for projects that you may handle alone as well as when leading a team. Business management is not complicated; it requires the discipline to plan, act and follow through in pursuing the goals of your business.

Action Items:

Use the flow-cycle for information handling to address the next issue your business faces. Practice using the systematic format until it becomes second nature.

Session 8
Organize for Results

You don't think you have time to organize? Guess What?—You're Right!

But you _really_ don't have the time **not** to! I doubt that anyone reading this book would fail to check the oil level in their vehicle because they "don't have the time"; we recognize the potential down-side later versus a couple of minutes now. The same goes for the development and use of proper management practices. You're running a business and you know more about running your business than anyone else. Take the time now to begin putting "what you know" and "what you do" into a structured process for running your business…and if you already have the structure in place, decide now on the adjustments you can make to improve the way the business runs.

Reflection

Today is a good time to reflect on your performance against your goals and to commit to paper your goals and plan of action for the next business period. Session 7, addressed the handling of information. Use the "measure-report-adjust" cycle of that guideline as a process for evaluating the results of your efforts. You've done the most difficult part in getting actions planned and started. Now, it's your responsibility as the business leader to take the time to fine-tune the execution of the plan.

Vision—Strategy—Execution (ViStrEx)

Successful business management is comprised of three integrated primary elements—Vision, Strategy and Execution. The reflection process, while part of the *Execution* phase, is closely coupled with the other two. As you evaluate your results and analyze the causes, test to ensure that the *Vision* is still valid and attainable and the *Strategies* are still "right" and timely. If not, define where the variances occur and why, gather the pertinent up-dated information and adjust either the *Vision*, *Strategy* or both to improve your probability of success. (Remember, *Tactics* and *Action Items* are part of the *Strategy*)

Consider your Business Plan to be a "living document"; work with it and adjust it to keep it current with your business environment.

Keep these thoughts in mind:

- The competitive environment is continually changing; you cannot stand still

- Nothing happens in a vacuum; all actions—and failures to act—have consequences; intended and un-intended

- There are things you can influence and things you cannot; know the difference

"Shifting Gears"

To this point, these Sessions have focused on presenting business management principles in a tutorial format, using "common sense" guidelines from my perspective, to trigger your ideas for implementation. I probably have not introduced anything you didn't already know, but perhaps I brought a different perspective to stimulate your thinking.

My goal has been to provide management tools that you can use to improve your business results. There will always be variations to present, but to be of higher value to you, the next few Sessions will be in Q&A format.

For the next few Sessions, I'll take the opportunity to promote my version of a disciplined, balanced approach to managing business.

Action Items:

Review where you stand against your goals. If you haven't written them, write three goals down now.

Session 9
Establishing and Using Business Metrics

Shifting Format

As mentioned in Session 8, we will shift into a "Q&A" mode to bring higher practical value by focusing on application of the principles to issues facing your businesses.

Execution of the Plan

Those reading this book recognize (I hope) that my focus is on accomplishing results. I try to go beyond stating the management principles and try to give the reader some specific, simple action steps to carry it out. I work to maintain the balance in addressing: 1) the selection and 2) the use of the management tools in our "toolbox." As in most jobs, there are various tools at our disposal; we use our judgment to choose the "right tool for the job" and rely on our training to use the tool properly. In management the greater challenge is in the execution or use of the "tool" rather than in the selection. I have seen studies that conclude that 80% of program failures are due to shortcomings in the execution of the plan. Management is a continuing exercise in the application of judgment and discipline. Stick with it; practice may not make perfect, but it will improve the probability of success.

Real Applications

As I wrote in Session 8, we'll shift to a "Q & A" format to better address actual implementation guidelines. Keep in mind, there is generally no single path to the goal but some are better than others and offer higher probability of success. I know of no suitable alternative to disciplining yourself to plan, follow-through, measure and adjust. (Refer to the "Information Handling" diagram in Session 7)

Where's the Leak?

"I get a monthly financial report from my accountant and for the past four months see my net income dropping. How do I find out what the problem is?"—Les

Les, I submit to you the *real* problem is that you haven't developed and implemented a disciplined financial management system. As urgently as you want to fight this fire, you need to invest the time now to develop the systems and procedures that will give you the financial data necessary to manage your business. This tool will not only enable you to identify the source of your current problems, but routine use will also help you to spot problem areas as they develop and to measure the effects of your actions. It's not complicated; just take it step-by-step and stick with it.

Here's the Fix

Step 1:   Prepare a budget
Use your records of past expenses and sales to develop a forecast of expected revenues and expenses. Use records only from as far back as is representative of current conditions and project only as far into the future as is reasonable.

Step 2:   Analyze the data
            Study the cash flow for each category of the budget and identify
            those areas that seem out of line.

Step 3:   Prioritize based on:

            • Where you can most easily cause change

            • Where you get the biggest "bang-for-the-buck"

Step 4:   Plan your action steps
            List the actions you will take to cause change in the areas you pri-
            oritized in Step 2. Be sure to include a timeline with completion
            dates.

Step 5:   Carry out your plan

Step 6:   Measure the results
            On a regular basis, either weekly or monthly, review your actual
            results against your budget

Step 7:   Document the results
            Write a report on the results, even if you are the only one who will
            see it.

Step 8:   Adjust

Step 8+:   Continue to measure, report and adjust until you have reached
           your goals.

Ok, so this is too simple; but using a "checklist" like this is effective. Pilots use simple checklists for a reason. You are piloting your business. Use the right tool and you'll have more fun reaching your destination.

Action Items:

Carry out Steps 1, 2 and 3 before this week ends. Start on 4 through 8 next week.

Session 10
Hiring the Right People

Missed a Step

"Mel, back in Session 3, you said it was the manager's responsibility to have the "right" people in key positions. Sounds good…but I'm just ramping my business up and don't know how I select the "right" person to hire. How do I go about this? I re-read your article but still don't know the first step. What do I do?".… Dave

You Need a Framework

You're right, Dave. I just re-read the article and get your point; guess I skipped the first step. I'll fix that now…and to control your expectations, I emphasize that I think this is the area of business management that calls for the greatest level of judgment. I know of no "magic bullets" or fixed rules, but there are some guidelines that help structure the process and improve the probability of successfully filling a position. Take the time to do this properly, with forethought, preparation and follow-through. A mistake in hiring is costly to fix.

The heart of your question is "How do you predict which candidate has the greatest probability of success in this position?" As I said, there are no guarantees, but with diligence and practice, you can develop a process that will provide a basis for your hiring decisions. Here are some ideas for developing a process that works for you. Keep in mind the candidate's skills, knowledge and ability to work with you and your organization.

Step-by-Step

Let's say you have written the position description, established the position level and compensation range and defined the metrics by which you will measure performance. You need those regardless of whether you are transferring a current employee into this position or hiring someone. Now you're ready to fill a position.

Step 1:   **Finding candidates**
Where is the pool of talent from where you will recruit? Think about how you will get the word out—your professional network, your employees (sometimes), industry associations, trade journals, newspaper, the internet, your competition, your suppliers are all good sources—then solicit résumés.

Step 2:   **Classifying candidates**
The résumé is the candidate's ticket for consideration; use recent performance reviews for current employees. Do an initial screening and segregate into "A", "B" and "other" groupings. Use your judgment in this step; communication is key in most jobs. Read between the lines; how and what is the candidate communicating? Do you quickly understand the qualifications, experience and career goals?

Step 3:   **Telephone screening**
Before starting the telephone screening, set up a matrix containing the important qualities/skills for the position and establish initial rankings based on their résumés. I find a scale of 1 to 5 works well. Start calling the highest scorers. During the phone call you can establish availability, interest, travel time (if appropriate) and determine verbal communication skills. Include these in the matrix.

Step 4:   **Face-to-face Interviewing**
Schedule the top scorers in the "A" group (start with six to ten) for a personal interview. Have your questions prepared and makes notes immediately following the interview and complete the rating of items in the matrix.

Step 5:   **Second Interview**
If you have viable candidates, invite them back for a second interview and arrange short meetings with others on your staff. (If you are not satisfied with the candidates so far, go back to your matrix, conduct the phone interviews and schedule the next set of candidates for personal interviews.)

Step 6:   **Final Exam**
Following the second interview, ask the top three to submit their plan of how they will, if selected, hit the ground running and come up to speed in the shortest time. Don't suggest any particular format for this. This step helps to determine their ability to:

• Comprehend what you have revealed about your business and the job

• Think and formulate a plan

• Communicate the plan

Step 6+:   **Job offer and Follow-through**

Make your selection and extend the offer. Consider your perception of how well you can work together. Meet regularly with the new employee. Ensure your expectations are understood and resources available to meet them. Provide feedback and manage progress.

Remember, these are guidelines. You'll need to adjust them to meet your particular situation.

Action Items:

Review your most recent hiring experience. Incorporate steps as needed to upgrade your hiring process.

Session 11
Running a Product
Development Program

The Balance between Focus and Opportunistic Effort

Frank called and said, "I've been developing a new product for about three months and now see variations that can open up other markets for me. What do I do? I can't chase all the opportunities at once, but don't want to let them slip by and my primary effort is taking most of my time."

Nice Problem

This is the kind of problem managers dream about, Frank…and your recognition that you can't pursue all opportunities at once tells me you see the challenge. If you've read previous Sessions, you know "judgment" and "balance" are cornerstones of management…and both will be necessary for you to manage this. You mentioned you are three months into your development program. I don't know the timeline for your program, but let's say you are at the stage where you are "tweaking" the design or formulation of the product and have received initial feedback from your "Beta" testers. You're right; your challenge is to meet the expectations of those already evaluating your product and simultaneously find a way to explore other opportunities. You need a process to help in the allocation of resources.

The Roadmap

Your first step will be to clearly state your goals. This will help you "see" what you really want; then you can evaluate your options for achieving the goal. The watchword at this stage is "simplicity." Keep it simple to help maintain your focus. Now put your development plan on paper.

Phase 1:   **Identifying Opportunities**
List the market opportunity for the primary product and all the others to be addressed by the variations. Now list all your resources and estimate the effort, resources and timeline for each.

Phase 2:   **Ranking Opportunities**
Recognizing that you cannot be all things to all people and you do not have unlimited resources, rank each opportunity considering the following example. This will help in your decisions. Working with so many units of measurement, a good technique is to use a 1 to 5 ranking system, 5 being "Best", assigning ranges with each criteria to "1", "2" etc. For example, say "time-to-market" of less than 3 months = 5; 3 to 6 months = 4 and so on. Select similar ranges for the other areas considered. Total your numbers and allocate your resources starting with the best opportunity (the highest score).

- Estimated time-to-market
  - 3 to 6 months–5
  - 6 to 12 months–4
  - 12 to 18 months–3

- Estimated development costs
  - $5,000–5
  - $10,000–4
  - $15,000–3
  - $25,000–2
  - $50,000–1

- Probability of success
  - 80%–5
  - 60%–4
  - 50%–1

- Sales projections (first year)
  - $1,000,000–5
  - $500,000–4
  - $250,000–3
  - <$250,000–1

- Earnings projections (first year)
  - 60%–5
  - 50%–4
  - 40%–3
  - 30%–2
  - 20%–1

- Projected break-even point
  - 12 months–5
  - 24 months–4
  - 36 months–1

Criteria	Opportunity #1—Initial	Opportunity #2	Opportunity #3	Opportunity #4
Time-to-market	4	3	5	4
Development Costs	2	3	5	4
Probability of Success	5	1	4	4
Sales	4	5	3	3
Earnings	3	2	1	4

Break-even	4	5	1	4
Total	22	18	19	23

Based on above, develop a plan to pursue "Opportunities #4 and #1." Measure results against your estimates and be prepared to re-allocate resources.

Phase 3: **Development of Prototypes**
Assign the development responsibilities, identify the milestones and meet regularly to monitor the progress of each development program. Ensure all deliverables are met before advancing to the next development step. Recognize "show-stoppers" and prudently reassign resources to other opportunities as missed key milestones occur.

Phase 4: **Finalization & Refinement of Offering**
Ensure the offering can be produced consistently, within specifications and budget. Get customer feedback from early production units and make adjustments as needed

Phase 5: **Resources for Commercialization**
Critically evaluate the sales, production, customer support and distribution resources and processes to ensure consistent supply to the customers. Plan and manage the market introduction based on your ability to supply.

Phase 6: **Roll-out**
Introduce to markets in a manner that allows you to maintain control. Decide if the market introduction will be a "blitz" or a "phased introduction" by market segment, regionally or some other criteria. Balance this with your resources.

Ongoing: **Product Management**
            Now arrange for ongoing management. Track where each
            offering in the product-line is in its life cycle and its contribu-
            tion to earnings. Compare results with your estimates made in
            Phase 2.

   The important message here is to adopt a logical process and instill the discipline in yourself and in your organization to follow the process and to adjust
and refine as conditions change and you gain market intelligence.

Action Items:

List three new opportunities and "rate and rank" them as described. Allocate
resources to those having the highest probability of success.

Session 12
Selecting a Board of Advisors

Every Manager Needs Some Help Sometime

Greg has a nice business, coming up on the fifth anniversary and really getting recognition in his targeted market…and with the success comes a new level of issues requiring decisions and action. The things keeping him awake at night lately include personnel decisions, contract negotiations, production expansion, sales literature and software purchases. Sound familiar? They should; they're typical for almost any business. But Greg is overwhelmed. He needs to arrange for some support. I have been working with him for about two years and have recommended that he establish a group of advisors to help with his management decisions. He kept putting me off, saying he wasn't ready (he was concerned about "losing face" by admitting he needed help)…until now…and now his need is "urgent" and he is slipping into the reactive mode. (Which we all know is counter-productive, right?)

In addressing this situation, I'll try to make present my comments in very general terms, as I recognize the readers of this column are involved in diverse business situations. But the basis for my comments is that you are the captain of your ship and you need a crew to help sail it to your intended port.

You're Still the Decision-Maker

Most managers, whether running a strategic business unit of a major corporation or their own small business, need a "support group", apart from their operational staff, where they can openly discuss issues and get advice. Some wise observer has said "Good business managers can do anything; they just can't do everything." Delegation and having a resource for information and guidance are two key tools for running a business. There are plenty of examples to demonstrate that the decisions of cross-functional teams are generally more effective than individual decisions. Look around—CEO's have a staff; Presidents have a Cabinet, Business Directors have a Business team; doesn't it make sense that you as a Business Manager have counsel available also?

You will continue to be accountable for the financial health of your business and by establishing such a team, you're not abdicating your responsibility for decision-making, but rather expanding your known options which you will consider in making your decision.

The Make-up

Regardless of your business situation and structure, I encourage you to establish such an advisory team. If you are part of a corporation, arrange for representatives from associated units to serve on your team...manufacturing, finance, HR, sales, R&D and marketing for example. If you have a "stand-alone" business, form your team from associates and colleagues, such as other business owners, your outside financial and legal firms, associates who are managers with major corporations and others who have demonstrated good judgment and success in business.

So, how do you arrange it? You will need "critical mass" to be effective. This is usually five to seven, plus yourself. Select people whom you trust and whose judgment your respect. Select members from a range of specific expertise but the most important quality you will need for an effective team is for each to have the personal chemistry to function as a team member.

Greg is now focusing on improving his skills in the design and running of his "Advisory Team" meetings. They currently meet every six weeks but plan to move to bi-monthly and then quarterly as they make progress in resolving issues and implementing the policies, systems and procedures. The meetings are "agenda-driven", limited to three hours and background information needed for discussion is distributed in advance. The purpose of the meetings is to provide Greg with suggested options, not to communicate information...this is done through outside channels.

Action Items:

List five people whom you would like to have as an advisory team. Over the next three weeks, explore the possibility with them.

Session 13
Measuring your Progress against Goals

Where are you today in the key areas that affect your business?

Are you on track? The right answer is either "Yes" or "No"…and you should have answered without hesitation. You as the business manager *must* know the answer to that…and measuring the performance of your business should be a continual effort and as natural as anything else you do.

- Where are you against your goals?

- If you're behind, what actions can you take to get on track?

- If you're ahead, can you improve the performance of your business by re-allocating resources?

This is a good time to break from our usual Q&A format and evaluate where your business stands. Look at the results of your most recent full quarter. This Session will continue to be Q&A, but this Session *I'll* ask the questions and perhaps they will stimulate you to look at your business from a different perspective. This isn't very sophisticated; it's really getting back to the basic ABC's, but it's an effective tool for staying grounded in reality.

Let's look at your year-to-date progress, define areas where action is needed and project expected milestones along the path to your goals. I trust your roadmap for the year is at hand with all plans, goals and programs compiled into one folder—either hard-copy or electronic file. It's also useful to have a summary sheet at the front for charting your progress. If it's not, prepare it now. This is a suggested framework. You may already be using different tools; if not, use these as a starting point and modify to suit your business and style.

Check-up

I expect your plans for the year included goals for most areas of your business; look at where you stand against your goals in:

- Financials
  - What are your earnings versus goal?
  - What are your revenues versus goal?
  - What are your costs versus goal?
  - What business metrics are you regularly measuring?
    - Revenue per employee?
    - Items sold per employee?
- People
  - How many employees have completed training as scheduled?
  - How many performance reviews have been conducted as scheduled?
  - What is your succession plan for your key people?
    - Is it current? If not, what action must you take?
- Offering
  - How many new products/services have you introduced?
  - How many products/services have you discontinued?
  - What new products/services are under development?
    - Are they on schedule?

- Customers
    - How many customers provide 80% of your sales?
        - Who are they?
        - Are there any threats to your business here?
    - How many customers provide 80% of your earnings?
        - Who are they?
        - Are there any threats to your business here?
    - What new products/services are under development?
        - Are they on schedule?
- Market
    - What is your market share?
    - What is your opportunity?
    - What is the total potential?
    - What new business can you get from current customers?
    - How many new customers have you targeted for 2003?
        - How many have your sales people visited so far?
- Operations
    - What are your fixed costs versus goal?
    - What are your variable costs versus goal?
    - What is your capital investment versus goal?

Tune-up

After evaluating actual year-to-date results versus planned and determining the difference, consider what actions you can initiate that will have the greatest probability of moving the business to your intended goals. Recognize the "importance hierarchy" of these results. That is to say, meeting your earnings targets takes precedence over being on schedule in conducting performance reviews. Maintain your "balance." This is the execution part, you've gathered your data and distilled it into usable information…now act on it, measure the results—say at end of this Quarter—and adjust as needed for the next Quarter.

Action Items:

Review the metrics by which you make decisions. If you don't have them established, start a list of what you think the key measurements are…test them for the next two months and revise as needed.

Session 14
The Competitive
Environment—Part I

How do you compare to your competitors?

Situational Awareness

Fighter pilots must intuitively have "situational awareness" (SA) to survive. They are truly a special breed. They must know the location and condition of other airborne forces—friendly and un-friendly—the ground forces—where are the good guys—the weather, fuel, ammunition and a lot of other stuff. On a different level, you as business managers also must work on developing your awareness of those things that can impact your businesses, and possibly, your survival. Let's think some of the elements in your arena. You, too, have allies—suppliers, distributors and customers—to list a few. And you have "un-friendlies", too—the competition…and when you consider your competition, think about the "not-in-kind" as well as "in-kind." Keep an eye on technology trends at the same time…don't be caught by surprise. Develop your "early warning radar systems" to keep you informed.

SWOT

Strengths, weaknesses, opportunities, threats—these are the primary targets in your analysis of the competitive environment. How will you gather the market intelligence to know where you stand? Start with your "allies." These are the people who want you to succeed. Your customers want good suppliers and they are eager to tell you how you can serve them better....BUT YOU'VE GOT TO ASK!...only a special few will volunteer that information. Too many will just check out your competition.

As in many other areas of business, your "feeling" is only a starting point. Now make a plan and timeline for collecting data and getting started. Compile this into a matrix or spreadsheet so you can rank your business against the competition. You can use this information later to embark on programs that capitalize on your strengths, allows you to improve your weak points and to attack those of your competition.

What are the "top" things your customers value? If you don't know, ask them...and while you've got their attention, find out how they prioritize them. Your quality customers will understand you are gathering this information so you can be a better supplier to them and will be willing to share this with you.

After identifying the top eight or ten, you want to find out how you compare in each of these against the best with whom your customers do business. This exercise will be more effective if you have the customer expand the universe to include <u>all suppliers</u>, not only your competition. This is the tricky part. People are generally nice and while they want to help you (and themselves) they don't want to hurt your feelings. So, a good approach to this potential hurdle is to arrange for a third party to interview your customers. Assure the customers that no specific statement will be attributed to a specific customer, but that the agglomerated information will be presented to you for actions to improve your service.

Performance Profile

Let's say you've settled on eight areas that your customers value highly: quality, communication, price, delivery time, breadth of offering, problem handling, ease of doing business and innovation. Now have your interviewer ask each customer to rate you in each of these areas using a scale of 1 to 10—10 being FANTASTIC. Then have them rate the best supplier in the same areas. Calculate the averages of each of these groupings and see where you fit. I like to plot these so I have a graphic display. In the example below, you can quickly see your weak points are "innovation" and "breadth of offering." You're "easy to do business with" including "communicating" and "handling problems" but if you don't have up-to-date offerings you face the threat of being "obsoleted" out of the market. This example raises red flags. Now re-visit your strategic plan and determine how you re-direct your business offering so you remain a viable and competitive supplier.

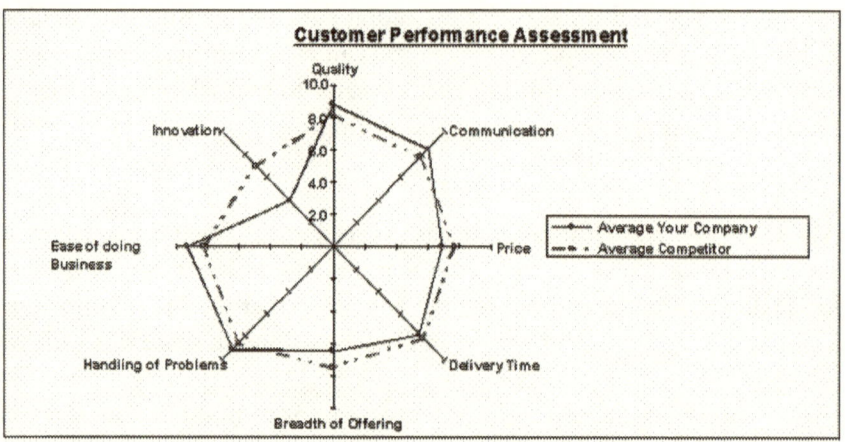

My word-counter tells me I'll have to leave some open issues for another Session. But here's a heads-up for you...

- How will you decide how many and which customers to survey?

- Are you prepared to act on the information you receive? You'd better; they will expect it.

- When will you have a follow-up to measure the effects of any changes you make?

Action Items:

List the top ten things you think are most important to your customers. Bounce them off a couple of your best customers as a sanity-check.

Session 15
The Competitive
Environment—Part II

Application and Use of the Customer Survey

Recap

In Session 14, I addressed the concept of conducting a customer survey as a business tool to improve your SA (situational awareness) and I left the readers with some un-answered questions. Let's wrap them up in this Session. The survey consisted of getting customers' perceptions of your performance in key areas versus the performance of the best of all their suppliers in each of those areas; the purpose being to improve your performance as a preferred supplier.

Getting Started

Several steps in this process require good thinking in order to make this exercise useful. Think carefully about these before you even start.

1. What will you measure?

2. How will you decide how many and which customers to survey?

3. Are you prepared to act on the information you receive?—you'd better; they'll expect it.

4. When will you have a follow-up survey to measure the effects of any changes you make?

You must resolve the first two items before launching the survey:

1) What to measure?

Canvass your organization (those who have contact with the customers) and select eight to ten areas as discussed in Session 14. Bounce these off the decision-makers at a few customers as a sanity check. Be organized and phrase your questions so the entire survey can be done in about ten minutes. For example, "On a scale of 1 to 10, how do you rate us on `ease of doing business'?" and "Using the same criteria, how do you rate your supplier who is the best in `ease of doing business'"? Calculate the average of all these responses and create a chart or diagram as shown in Session 14.

2) Who to survey?

Don't give in to the temptation to survey your favorite customers...go for a representative cross-section of your customer base. Don't try to understand their rationale now...we're dealing with perceptions at this point...just get their initial feeling about your performance level. You'll collect facts in later steps. Ideally, you'd want to include all those customers in the 20% who generate 80% of your business, but use your common sense and select a reasonable number that'll be enough to generate meaningful results.

OK, so let's say you've worked your way through items 1 and 2 and have now completed the survey. Here's the really important part...the reason you did this in the first place...how will you use the information?

Survey Results and Your Strategic Plan

3) Now let's think about your next steps...the real execution part...and remember *execution* is the phase of management where most failures occur.

By the very fact you've asked the questions, you've raised expectations in the minds of your customers. They think you'll do something that will benefit them. We touched on the need to *"control expectations"* some Sessions back; (see Sessions 3,4,10 and 11) this is an important time to keep that principle in mind. What will you do? How can you use this information...consistent with your strategic plan...to improve you position in the marketplace?

Analyze the survey results for areas where you can take action that will capitalize on your strengths and minimize your weaknesses. Act first on those areas where you'll get the greatest return for your efforts. Strategize with your field and operational staff on specific actions that will impact the customers' perceptions of your competence and value as a supplier. Start with those that interact with your customers, get their suggestions, then meet with your support people and see what can be done to change those areas you've targeted. Use the timelines and accountability guidelines we've addressed in previous Sessions.

4) You owe it to those surveyed to provide some level of feedback. They agreed to help you expecting that you would use the information to become a better supplier to them…in other words "to make their life easier." Decide on the timing for a follow-up survey. Ensure the timeliness by giving yourself enough time after implementation of the changes for the customer to have "felt" the improvement; but don't wait so long as to lose the momentum of the program. Have your facts ready for the follow-up…be prepared to show improvement in specific areas that were rated in the survey. Keep everyone up to date with the program. Figure out some charts you can post in the parts of your business that affect specific items on the survey and plot your internal performance for all to see. Share this with your customers.

Another principle you'll need to keep in mind is *"balance."* There are many judgment calls in this process. Strive to avoid extremes in each part of the process. This is a useful tool to help you reach your goals; it is not itself the goal.

Action Items:

Arrange for someone to survey your key customers according to this process.

Session 16
A Snapshot of your Business

An Introspective Exercise

"Good managers know their limitations." Dirty Harry (with literary liberties)

Over the Sessions, we've addressed many different areas of business management that require the attention of the person accountable for the financial health of that business. I've written of the need for the business manager to practice "situational awareness" (SA in the jargon of pilots). This term applies to the entire constellation that may affect the business—your offering, competitive threats, demographic changes, resources, currencies and regional economies to list a few. You must know where you stand and know your capabilities in these areas. I've also addressed business tools that you can use to evaluate, focus and prioritize in order to be able to handle the most important.

In Sessions 14 and 15, we've looked at techniques and tools to measure the perception our customers hold of our performance—a look from the "outside." This Session let's look at where your business stands from your perspective—a look from the "inside." What is **your** perception of your business? Pull your business plan out and look critically at your goals for the next two years. Do you currently have in place the policies, systems, procedures and resources necessary to achieve the goals? This will help you to define your limitations. You'll still have surprises, but this will help minimize them…both in frequency and severity.

This exercise calls for a real dose of "objectivity." Ideally, you will undertake this with your staff or business team. If that isn't practical, I suggest that you get a second opinion from another person who knows your business and your goals.

Getting Started

Let's continue using our rating scale of 1 to 5 to rate your business in this exercise…and let's look at two time-frames—today and some mid-point, say, two years hence. Your next step is to identify the critical business areas of your business—select the top twenty or so. This list should help get started:

- Production Process
- Production Staff
- Production Facility
- Product Offering
- Pricing Structure
- Purchasing
- Payroll

- Financial Reports
- AP/AR procedures
- Maintenance
- Management Staff
- The Planning Process
- Execution Capability
- Succession plans

- Acquisition targets
- Documented Policies, Systems & Procedures
- Sales
- Distribution
- Marketing

Evaluate the capability of your business to handle each of the areas effectively.

- Do you have the appropriate infrastructure in place now?
- Will it be capable of handling the projected business?
- If not, how can you develop or acquire the needed skills and assets?

Drill Down

Critically analyze each selected area. Here are some ideas to lubricate the brain gears and get them turning freely…expand on these basic starters. For example, for each area on my list above, ask yourself questions such as:

- Are your production processes robust and capable of ensuring on-going quality?

- Is your production staff adequate and qualified?

- Will your facility handle the projected volumes?

- Are you prepared to manage your product offering with new product development and product phase-out under control?

- Does your pricing policy incorporate standard pricing with flexibility for special pricing with appropriate controls?

- Do you have enough qualified people to handle purchasing, payroll, financial reporting, accounts payable and accounts receivable?

- Do you have preventative maintenance programs in place?

- Do you have the "right" people in the key positions of your management team?

- Do you have a strategic planning process in place?

- How well do you execute your plans?

- Do you have a process for grooming successors to those in key positions?

- Are you going to grow organically only, or is an acquisition appropriate?

- Are your policies, systems and procedures well documented, up-to-date and communicated adequately?

- Are your sales, distribution and marketing plans and organizations in place?

As usual for me, I find it helps to show the results graphically with something like the following chart. I suggest any area rated less than three is not adequate to carry out your mission. Your job is to fix those areas…or find ways to compensate.

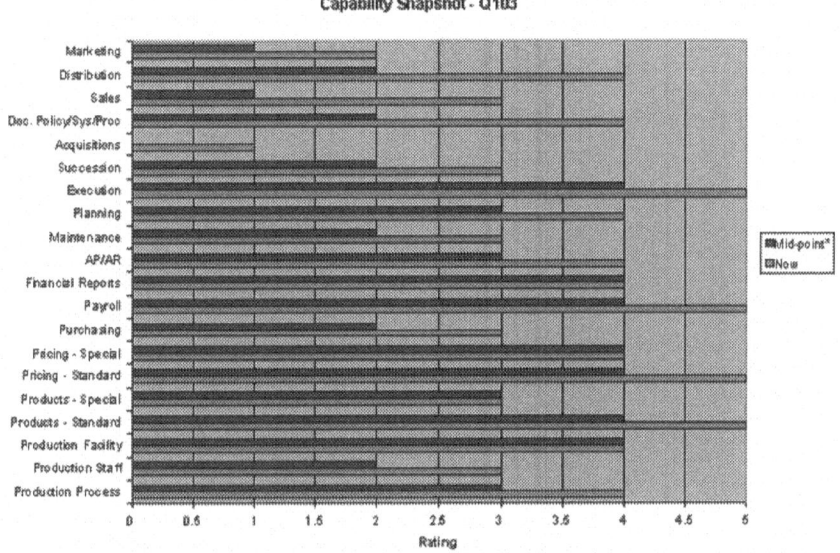

Capability Snapshot - Q103

How does your situation look? What needs attention now? What needs to be strengthened for the mid-point? Go back to the questions you asked in your drill-down exercise and develop programs to correct any deficiencies.

Action Items:

Take a snapshot of your business. Ask those on your staff to do likewise. Compare and evaluate results.

Session 17
Plan, Execute & Follow-through

Don't Complicate Your Business

One of my colleagues recently wrote to me, "When it comes to good marketing and good management much of it is common sense and that makes your (writing) job very difficult, because everyone knows the answers, but never knows how to implement and get results." I agree wholeheartedly. I doubt you will read anything in these columns that you haven't heard or didn't know. My objective is to provide another perspective, a reminder, some specific tool or merely the encouragement to drive on and "make it happen." With these thoughts in mind, I offer this Session's exercise—follow what your common sense tells you and, most importantly, *act on it!*

Business isn't complicated—though we often complicate it through our actions and failures to act. Think about it…every manager has experienced the results of un-intended consequences.

No question, most of our businesses are complex, but I think that's different. Complex things are manageable…just break them into the basic elements. I say complicated things are disorganized…you must fix that first. Think of "complicated" as "chaos" and think of "complex" as "matrix-organized." Consider a symphony, a complex piece of work, but the conductors and the musicians produce beautiful music.

Einstein said, "*Everything must be made as simple as possible, but not one bit simpler.*" I sure can't improve on this. Make this your goal.

Use the management tools at your disposal to achieve this and;

- **Plan Flexibly**
- **Execute Decisively**
- **Follow-through Diligently**

Managing with these watchwords in mind will help achieve the *clarity of purpose* necessary to lead your business.

Flexible Planning

Here I go again on the importance of *balance* in all that you do. Yes, I believe you must have a plan…and you must follow it. But make sure your plan includes provisions for handling potential "what-ifs" and opportunistic situations. But don't follow it blindly. Keep your antennae out to detect changes in your business universe and make adjustments accordingly. Seek the balance between "staying the course" and adjusting for reality. Heartily resist changing your strategy, but readily accept the need for necessary changes in your tactics. Know the difference between nimbleness and wishy-washy and act accordingly. Your people can tell the difference and their support will be proportional to their belief in your leadership. There's a lot of truth in the adage "The better I plan, the luckier I get."

Decisive Execution

Preparation is the first step to confidence. If you've developed your plan and provided for contingencies, you should confidently act on the plan. Remind yourself of the qualities and characteristics of leaders who have inspired you and practice adopting their actions to your style. You can be sure you'll make some mistakes…only those who do nothing make no mistakes…but with a good plan as foundation, you can recover with a minimum loss. Execute your plan with the belief that your goals are realistic and attainable and really understand what is within your control and what is not. Act on the best information available; as you gain new information, adjust consistent with your strategy. Be proactive in addressing the key issues and provide resources and back-up tactics to respond to those things beyond your control.

Diligent Follow-through

The Prussian general and military strategist Karl von Clausewitz, (1780-1831) is quoted as saying that `no war plan withstands the first actions of battle´. Recently others have applied this comment to business and have equated business to war. I interpret this thought as, "managers (and generals) must develop their own strategic judgment in order to handle the fluid environment of the business arena." In Session 14, I wrote about "situational awareness." SA is a necessary part of proper follow-through. Coupled with measurement against goals as a continual process, it provides an effective framework for managing.

Remember Einstein's admonition—test the limits of simplification. If you over-simplify, consider that part of the learning process and re-adjust until it works. Persistence and the discipline to measure results are necessary in managing and will bring rewards.

Action Items:

List three key things that affect your business that are not within your control. Write down some actions you can take to minimize any negative impact.

Session 18
Be Alert for Good Ideas

Managing and Managing

In Sessions 5 and 6, I wrote about my belief in the need for business managers to be aware of where they spend their time…the three modes of "Managing" being *planning, leading and managing*. Managers must not only be competent in all, but they must manage themselves to control how much time they spend in each. Critically evaluate what you do and ask yourself, "Does this need doing for the good of the business and am I the one who should be doing it?" But remember the balance aspect…there are some things that only you as the Manager can do effectively, even if you would prefer to delegate. Self-management is a key factor impacting your success as a Manager. Here's the take-away: *Don't expect to manage others until you can manage yourself.*

Hidden Pearls

This has been brought home to me recently from some unexpected sources…NASCAR and Formula One. I catch a few races and enjoy not only the excitement of the race, but also trying to figure out the team strategies and watching the execution. And occasionally I get a bonus idea or two from the interviews. Hidden amongst the boilerplate that drivers quote about sponsors and team effort, a couple of principles from the "little m" management toolbox jumped out at me. Perhaps some of you readers heard this and were impressed also. I've heard crew-chiefs and mechanics refer to the drivers as the "spacer"—that thing separates the steering wheel and the seat. But these guys do more than drive the car. Think about the following interview interactions and how you can apply the concepts to your management philosophy.

NASCAR's Dale Earnhardt Jr., when asked about a mistake in the pits, said that soon after it happened he made it a point to talk with the pit-crew about putting the incident behind them…learn from it and move on. "We have to create a situation where they (the pit-crew) can set goals for tomorrow (race day)…not just try to get through the day."
Wow…how often do we see business managers failing in that area?

During Qualifying, Formula One's Michael Schumacher, despite a driving mistake, took the pole. The interviewer expressed surprise and asked how he had overcome the error and made up the lost time. Schumacher's response; "You can't do anything about what has happened…you must do what you can to manage what lies ahead."
Another gem! How often must we remind ourselves of that?

Note a couple of points here; 1) the situations involved a mental outlook and 2) the managers, in this case, the drivers, took appropriate and immediate action. Granted, we don't normally have the reward of immediate results for our efforts as these guys did but the management responsibility is there just the same and we are all paid for results.

Keep Your Antennae Out

Here's the second take-away for the Session; *Practice looking for management ideas and tools in your daily non-business life.* Guess what! It may be non-business for you, but it's very much business for someone. Opportunities to learn abound in all kinds of situations. Practice looking in venues un-related to your business for little gems of thinking. Learn from what other successful people do and adapt and adopt for your business needs. One of the skills I value most highly is the ability to recognize good practices, seek the underlying principle and apply it to an un-related field.

Putting into Practice

I once overheard Mario Andretti comment about a fellow driver, "He should know when to quit." He meant, of course, that he thought the other guy was past his prime and getting in the way of others. But we can apply that thought as a reminder that we need to measure everyone's performance, including ourselves, and adjust appropriately. And with that I see I've spent my allotted words.

Where have you found unexpected ideas or inspiration?

Action Items:

List some places where you have found "good ideas." Don't forget films such as "12 O'clock High" with Gregory Peck as the Squadron Commander. Keep a list of ideas and their source. This will help stimulate the process.

Session 19
Communications—Part I

Could Your Communications Be Improved?

This Session, let's really get back to the basics and, once again, this is a D-I-Y exercise. I present this only as a reminder for you to think about things you already know…then do a little analysis and work up ways to improve as you identify shortfalls.

I've written about various factors involved in managing your business, but the one "thing" that enables all these other "things" to work is *communication*. As a manager, most of what you accomplish is through the efforts of others…and we recognize others must believe in your ability to lead them and the business before they act with commitment. I believe the quality of your communications is the most basic of all skills needed for effective management…and to get others on board. They must clearly understand where you are leading them.

What'daya Think That Means?

Remember the skit about the nuclear power plant when the operator tells the apprentice, "You can't let this gauge get too high."?…and leaves. The needle starts moving up and the apprentice wonders, "Did he mean it doesn't matter how high it gets, or don't let it get too high?"—KABOOM!!

Maybe your communication issues aren't that critical...or perhaps they are. In any case, you have an obligation to others and to the business to communicate effectively.

There are some natural communicators amongst us, but most of us must work at it. It requires dedicated thought, effort and follow-up. How do you communicate...and how well do you do it? We all communicate daily, experience miscommunication and spend time correcting misperceptions and misunderstandings; but how much time or thought do we give to improving our communications...to making them more effective? Are you learning from your missteps? As an experiment, for the rest of today, work at being aware of your communication and the results...all of the signals you send...verbal, written, body language, what you respond to and what you ignore...everything people will receive and perceive. Then evaluate how you could have been more effective.

As the moving parts of our machines must operate in an environment of complete lubrication, the interacting parts of our businesses should also operate without friction. Think of the "communications culture" of a business as the "lubricants" necessary for the business functions to work smoothly.

You know, from either sad experience or the misfortune of others, the criticality of the proper lube for a machine—type, quantity, cleanliness and routine attention. Same goes for your business...and just as lubes are compounded for specific applications, so too should your communications be tailored for your business, and to each specific message.

Some Things to Consider

Think about it...behind most communicating is the need to manage expectations in some way. Effectively getting your message out and having it received as you want requires some forethought and preparation. Selecting the appropriate method of communication for a specific message is similar to selecting the correct lubricant for a particular machine application. You have a number of communications tools available and want to select the "right" one for each communications effort. Sometimes silence is the best mode of communication.

Understand clearly your intent and communicate appropriately. The purpose may be to:

- Educate/Inform
- Provide direction/instructions
- Cause actions
- Solicit information

Let's take a "bit of information" and walk through a thought process.

- Should this be communicated or not?—Which will be more beneficial for the business? Some things *should* be ignored, but you must know the difference.
    - If it should be communicated, who should be included?
- What format will be best
    - Verbal (personal, voice mail or video)
    - Written (hardcopy or e-mail)
    - Are there any persons or groups who should be given advance notice?

The primary objective of a lubrication system is to manage friction. There is "friction", too, as information passes through an organization. For our machines, we select, for example, oil or grease. Then we select the appropriate viscosity or load rating. Same for your communications, select the format, then the style.

Message Received?

Consider also the factors that may affect the receivers' understanding of what you are communicating. Then check—did they receive the message you intended to send? This is two-way—you send; others receive—there are filters and complications on both ends. A few things to consider:

- Language fluency/Comprehension
- Listening/reading skills
- Extent of background information
- Pre-conceptions/Expectations
- Interest or lack of

- Timing
- Other distractions such as, personal issues or business rumors

I make it a practice to solicit feedback from a representative sampling to evaluate the effectiveness of my messages. Try it—it's enlightening. Just be prepared for what you hear and don't get defensive. On that note, I welcome your comments.

Action Items:

Ask a "straight-shooting" colleague to comment on your latest communication. Select one area where you will work to improve in your next communication.

Session 20
Communications—Part II

Follow-up and Follow-through

Taking a dose of my own advice regarding flexible planning, follow-through, situational awareness and adjustment after measuring, I offer these additional thoughts. Consider these as an addendum to Session 19 on the leaders' communication responsibilities. Perhaps these ideas will be useful in your business communications. I'm aware that in some situations, the speaker wants to speak without saying anything, but in business communications, this is so transparent that your audience will lose respect either right then or later when they think about what they learned—or didn't learn—from you.

Watch What You Say!

I recently heard someone respond to a request for a report with, "I'll try to get that to you as soon as I can." Huh? What does that mean?…might as well have said, "Maybe I will and maybe I won't." Can the requestor count on getting *anything*?—And if so, when? I consider this a real disservice. Either say, "No, I cannot get that to you." Or say, "OK, you'll have it by next Tuesday." That way the requestor can take other appropriate action. Let people know what to expect.

Here's a goal for the next fiscal period—Make a commitment to work consciously on upgrading the effectiveness of your communications…and to fit within the scope of this column, I'll address only the "sending" half of *your* part. Your "receiving" part and the "sending" and "receiving" parts of your audience are important, too, however, considering my goal of establishing *you* in the minds of others as the person who knows where you are leading the business and how you will do it, I emphasize your "message sending" skills. It's easy to overlook the need to routinely evaluate how your communications are received…especially what *you* could have done to improve the results. However, this is another aspect of managing that is key in your goal of leading others. Remember, your success usually depends on how well your employees and others work toward the goals you have set. Next time you have the opportunity to communicate, pay attention to the words you use and then critically evaluate how they were received in the minds of your audience. People respect managers who are "straight shooters" and who "get it." "Clueless" managers are ridiculed…and that creates a real uphill battle for achieving your goals. Review you latest communication; how often did you use "weasel words"?…and under what circumstances?

Strive to communicate directly. "Later" may be an appropriate timeline under some circumstances, but usually people want to know *when*. If you can't be specific, say so…and explain either why you cannot specify or that you cannot address that topic now. Sometimes the right statement is, "I don't know now, but I expect to know by "x-date" and I'll let you know then."

…and Watch How You Say It

I was in a group addressed by several speakers, one of whom was Alan Shepard, one of the original seven astronauts; another was a well-known motivational speaker. During the break, I heard comments about how boring Shepard's talk was and how entertaining the motivator was. I remember thinking at the time about the importance of Shepard's message, and that his key points were lost on so many of the audience. That was their loss, his insights into discipline, planning, commitment and focus were dead-on; but think of how many more he could have gotten through to had he tailored his presentation to the audience.

The Fog of Communication

Which brings us to another consideration; what is the purpose of your communication?—to inform, to discuss or to converse? Posture yourself appropriately. When you're informing, make sure to minimize any vague comments and words so your audience has simple, clear points to take away. Discussions and conversations may be a little more informal, but still speak so your message gets through.

It's hard enough to get your message across in the most favorable situation. Recognize the things you can and cannot control and optimize what you can. All speakers have been misunderstood and misquoted. Expect some level of this and do what you can to minimize it.

TIME OUT: Case in point! I just fell into the trap of "vague words." Exactly what did I mean in the previous paragraph by "...*do what you can...*"? To be of any real use, I must specify some action steps to prepare beforehand, such as:

- Write out your objective so it's clear in your mind (Note: in doing this, you may realize you really have nothing to say or that you aren't properly prepared. So take care of this before proceeding with the following steps.)

- List key points

- List anticipated questions (and have responses)

- Define any desired follow-up actions

- Select conducive venue and timing

You Owe Your Listener

One of your fundamental obligations as leaders is to respect others. The words you choose in your communications shape your listeners' perceptions of your heartfelt feelings...consciously and subliminally. Plan and practice. Don't talk down to your audience...and take care that you don't speak over their heads either. Answer their questions or say you cannot. Don't leave it vague. Arrange for a colleague to review you communications. Remember, "off-the-cuff" comments are often the result of hours of much consideration and preparation.

Action Items:

Examine your latest communication for possible misinterpretation. Use your imagination. Then decide how you could have communicated with no questions as to your intent.

Session 21
Documentation

You Know the Basics are Important, so why not use Them More Often?

In Session 19, I referred to "really getting back to the basics" when I wrote about communicating. This Session I'll expand on the value of using basic business tools and guidelines, not only to help instill discipline and to produce more results, but for the added benefit of serving as a sanity check. I find that developing the conscious discipline of going back to the appropriate fundamental principle or guideline serves as a touchstone for your programs…sort of as pilots use their checklists before take-off.

My challenge in writing this is; "How can I best emphasize the effectiveness of using basic principles without over-stating the obvious?"

Your challenge in reading this is to find some useful tidbit in here and find a way to apply it to your management approach. You already know most of what I write; my job is to stimulate you to practice the discipline to apply that which you've learned about managing a business…and people.

A couple of incidents will help to get my point across and perhaps motivate you to review your business environment and your use of basic business tools critically.

I Really Don't Want to Do This

I recently experienced a valuable revelation while working with a new client. He has been in business for about fifteen years and brought me in to formalize a strategic plan for expanding his customer base and increasing revenues. I listened to what he said he wanted and laid out several strategies. As I played back to him what I heard him say he wanted, he had a real "ah-ha moment." He said, "I really don't want to do this business anymore. I want to do something different." We shifted focus and worked up two plans—one to phase out and shut down the existing business and another to launch a new business where his heart really is. As he saw me out he said, "Look at me…I'm smiling for the first time in a long time."

The point is he knew he wasn't doing what he wanted, but the discipline of documenting the goals and the key issues helped him "see" what he wanted. Going back to these basic tasks revealed what was hidden by his reactions to the day-to-day operations. Sometimes it takes an outsider to force this, but if you practice the introspective exercises that I wrote about a few Sessions ago, you can be your own mentor…at least up to some point. Practice listening to your inner-self. This is part of being "grounded" and is necessary for a satisfying career.

I Can't Do All This

A second incident further demonstrates the value of these basic procedures; in this case the client wanted to expand into two additional market segments in order to generate additional revenue streams to smooth out the seasonal effects of his primary market. Same drill; we established the goals, identified the key issues and when he evaluated the strategies and tactics necessary, he realized he would be too de-focused…and bringing on others to handle these tasks wasn't viable. We re-grouped and now have a strategic plan that focuses on growing the business in the primary market segment; he will expand into the new segments but with controlled, minimal effort and exposure. Preliminary results indicate he will achieve the revenue stabilization and remain focused on his primary business.

The real benefit in this case is that he has prevented the frustration of trying to do more than is reasonable. Seeing the potentials and the challenges on paper helped him clearly see what made sense.

Discipline and Accountability

I want your "take-aways" this Session to be *your* renewed commitment to work on:

- Improving your discipline to consistently use good, fundamental business tools and practices

- Holding yourself and other personally accountable for meeting commitments

I believe these are the cornerstones of your business management foundation. I'll present more on my management beliefs in following books.

Action Items:

Are you routinely using the tools we've discussed in this book? Meeting plans, action charts? Goal-setting? Measurement against goal? If not, re-dedicate yourself to this style of management now.

Session 22
Measuring your Milestones

It's Up To You

I spend a lot of time thinking about ways I can better get my points across in these articles...mostly trying to find the words that will inspire you to manage proactively. Doesn't matter how many times you read this article or what words I write; until you take the first actions to implement the "right" policies, systems or procedures into systematic use, I submit you are not fulfilling your management responsibilities and optimizing opportunities. My goal in writing this is to convince you to commit to work on improving your use of certain management tools.

Now's the Time

As you read this, there must be some milestone coming up for you...a new year, new month, new quarter, whatever. Set that as your re-start point and commit to taking some of the actions mentioned in this Session. Make a note to re-read this Session at your year-end, but to get your thinking prepared now's the time to take some quiet hours and review your accomplishments (and disappointments) for the previous time period. That's the first step...now follow up with analysis of any offsets. Why were results any greater or less than goal? Was it because of things within your control? Or due to outside factors? What steps can you take in the next period to improve your control and the results? What were your three most significant accomplishments in the previous period? Your three greatest disappointments? What can/should you do now?

Make this a comprehensive exercise; analyze all aspects of your business and take appropriate action to ensure improvements for the coming year. Do you feel you have your finger on the pulse of your business? Even if you answer "yes", chances are you can identify some area for improvement. Go through this exercise yourself first; later you can lead your staff and managers through it. You probably have some different points than I've listed here and I encourage you to modify this framework to fit your business culture. The important issue is to act. Let's get started…

#1—Personal Growth

How did you do in goals for yourself? Did you increase your knowledge in:

- Management techniques—how many books did you read? Did you participate in any seminars or training courses?

- Competitive threats—what did you learn about new technologies? What mergers & acquisitions are on the horizon?

- Key customer strategies—how will their future needs affect your relationship and business?

- Key supplier strategies—are they secure as suppliers? How will their plans affect your business?

- What areas will you work to improve in the next period?

Employees

What have you done to promote their loyalty?

- How many do you know by name? The names of their family members? Their interests? Important events in their lives?

- Did all employees receive a performance review?—people appreciate feedback. What are their goals?

- Do all employees understand the goals of the business?—do you inform them of progress against goals?

- How many employees participated in educational or training programs?

- Do you know how they feel about your business?

- What employee programs will you implement or expand on during next period?

Plans

- Did you meet your business goals?—financial? market share? new product development and roll-out?

- Do your plans include use of the key metrics for your business?—are there any better measurements?

- How often did you review and measure progress against your plan last year?—monthly, quarterly and annual are typically the minimums necessary for real progress.

- What are reasonable and attainable goals for next period?—don't just select some arbitrary increase over the previous period; evaluate the market environment and do a "ground-up" setting of goals.

Discipline and Accountability—re-visited

Last Session I encouraged you to focus on these two principles. The exercises outlined in this article present a convenient opportunity for you to practice these. On the theme "Management through Leadership", managers strive to inspire confidence in those on whom they depend to accomplish their goals. Paying attention and managing according to the framework presented here is an important step in that process. Take some time, seriously consider these things and ACT ON THEM; I believe that will help make future periods more successful.

Action Items:

Schedule "get-to-know" meetings with your key customers and key suppliers within the next six months.

Session 23
Your Management Style

Principles and Style

This session let's tie our exercise in management introspective to the use of additives in the formulation of engine oils for your car. Think of the **management principles** we address in these sessions as the base oil, and your **management style** as the additive package that makes it work. Imagine all the things involved as "the system"…whether it's a lube system or a management system.

There are some fundamental parallels…

- No matter how sophisticated the additive package, it won't get the job done without good base oil. Same with managing; style without sound principles isn't effective…not in the long run…often not even in the short run.

- Just as formulators develop the oil additive package considering not only the components to be included, but also the concentration of each, so too your managing style must be in balance. Your actions must "hang together" and make sense to others. You must consciously and consistently work on developing your leadership technique.

- Years ago—pre-1930—few lube systems required additives. Base oils alone worked fine then, but they wouldn't meet the performance demands of today. And years ago, managers' styles often were accepted without question because "they were the boss." Today the performance demands have increased for oils *and* managers. Today's business managers must be leaders…managers with the right balance of "style addi-tives." They must "formulate" their "package" to address the conditions that shape the conditions of their business world. So, how do they do that? No magic answer, but here are a few guidelines to help *you* develop your package. (Note the emphasis on "you.")

Be Yourself & Know Yourself

You know where to go to buy the materials for formulating an oil additive package, but what about the techniques that make up your "style package"? Where do you go for them? It's your responsibility to identify sources of knowledge and information. Dedicate time to continually grow in knowledge in your business and in the execution of your managerial responsibili-ties—read, attend conferences and seminars and in general learn from others, but it's crucial to be true to yourself. Don't try to copy someone else's style, but do adopt and adapt the positive things you observe to your way of doing things…and work to avoid the negative things. The bedrock of your manage-ment style must be *honor*, and the foundation blocks must be *discipline* and *accountability*. The other principles that are the building blocks of your busi-ness are built on these. Do your homework, know where you are taking your business and believe in your people and goals. Make sure you have a strategic plan and use it as your roadmap, updating on a regular basis so it reflects the current environment of your marketplace. Having that level of confidence enables you to maintain focus and balance.

What is your natural style of managing? Have you thought about it? Could you achieve better results using different techniques? Each of us can improve but we have to know how we behave now and what actions we want to mod-ify. The first step is to devote some time thinking about how you accomplish your management goals…understand how you interact with others and their perceptions of you and the things that are important to you.

It's an R&D Program

Formulators of oil additive packages use a disciplined product development program to find the balance of compounds that will make up their total pack-age. Their goal is to protect metal surfaces, expand the application range and extend the life of the lubricant. Their challenge is to find the right combination of anti-wear, anti-friction, anti-foaming, anti-oxidizing and anti-deposit agents, corrosion inhibitors, dispersants, viscosity modifiers and metal de-activators. Each must work with the base oil and with each other.

As a business manager, you face similar challenges in developing the style in which you execute your responsibilities. Your goal is to:

- Ensure the financial health of the business

- Provide growth opportunities for the employees

- Manage the life cycle of the product-line

Your challenge is to find the right mix of methods and techniques. Use the same program protocol for developing your management style that the formulators use in developing their additive packages. True, you are looking for intangibles whereas the formulators are seeking materials, but the search and evaluation procedures can be very similar. Identify viable sources, analyze each and test the most promising. There is a wide selection of books, seminars and Internet-based guides on recognizing your style and modifying as appropriate…but it's up to you to make it happen. The real difference between your program and that of the formulators is that yours must be ongoing. You have the un-ending challenge of making continuous improvements in your management style. Set your goals, measure your progress against them and adjust your actions as necessary. Along the way, test to confirm that your goals continue to be appropriate and re-set as the new facts indicate you should for the health of your business.

Action Items:

List three people you consider to be effective leaders and list their key characteristic. How does yours compare? Work to improve as indicated.

Session 24
Decision-making

Heads or Tails?—Call It!

You're a decision-maker—you set direction and choose courses of action, both proactive and reactive. That's what managers do...and the success of the business depends on the quality of your decisions. So, you don't just flip a coin or guess, you make decisions based on sound facts...when you can get them...and when you cannot, which is most of the time, you weigh the information and make a decision based on...what? Well, it depends...but bottom line is you must make judgments considering the accuracy of the "facts", the timing of actions, possible consequences and importance to your business.

One of the essentials of managing through leadership is the demonstrated and recognized ability to exercise good judgment. Now we're getting into the essence of management, and I don't have a short answer; but I will offer a few guidelines that may help you in your own program. There are no "one-size-fits-all" answers here, but I present a "framework for thinking" that you can adapt to your style and develop into a guide for your own consistent decision-making process.

Prioritize

Some decisions are "easy" in that the possible consequences, both intended and un-intended, won't significantly influence the business, either positively or negatively. Other decisions are important, in that the results can significantly affect the business. Some are urgent and require quick action; others have longer timelines. Learn to distinguish between important and urgent. A few—only a small percentage—will be both urgent and important. These are the challenges…and call for clear thinking and expeditious action. It is important to recognize these, establish the hierarchy of decisions and put the issue at hand into some "importance/relevance" category.

I've adapted a classification structure that one of my time-management coaches suggested for prioritizing tasks. His technique was to manage then by assigning each to one of four categories and taking appropriate action. I think the same classifications apply in responding to business events and situations.

Event/Situation Classification

- Not important—perhaps no action required

- Important—has potential to affect business strategy; requires judicious decisions and effective actions; recognize levels of importance and act accordingly

- Urgent—time sensitive; level of importance may be low, but delay in action may have increasing negative effect on business

- Urgent & Important—top priority; these become key issues and require immediate attention, planning, action, follow-up and adjusting

To classify as suggested, you must have information. But in the real world of running a business, how do you get the information on which you base your decisions? We've addressed acquiring and processing information in previous issues, so I won't plow that ground again this month. For review/clarification, refer to Session 9.

Sought After and Elusive Qualities

Leaders exhibit certain recognizable qualities. Two of these are "poise" and "good judgment." They come naturally to some and I believe all others can acquire and develop them through effort…but we must know in our hearts to the degree we possess each and decide if we see the value and really want to improve in these areas. I won't attempt in this column to tell you how to acquire poise or good judgment; that would be like one of those programs on "How to fake sincerity in 3 easy lessons"—it just doesn't work. What **will** work is taking steps to increase your confidence. Confidence comes from having clarity of purpose; having a well thought-out business plan and using it as your roadmap is one way to instill that confidence. A good plan is your touchstone for decision-making. Your principles, goals and strategies are recorded there.

"Balance" threads through all aspects of managing through leadership. Be aware of how you behave when making decisions. Conduct a self-critique after key events and adjust your actions appropriately.

- Avoid "knee-jerk" reactions and "paralysis through analysis"—find the middle ground

- Recognize when to stop gathering facts and when to start acting—know when you have adequate detail

- Make sure your actions support the vision, mission, goals and strategies of the business—this maintains your consistency

- Live and manage by your Operating Principles—honor is the bedrock of your actions

Practice Makes Perfect...Sometimes

Reality is, "practicing the right things, makes for improvement"...and you can improve your skills in these areas through resolve on your part to do it. Help yourself to grow in management skills by taking the time to reflect on situations, actions and results. Develop the resolve, perseverance and patience to evaluate the results against the desired results and adjust as needed to achieve your goals. What combination of things would have pushed the outcome more favorably? Were you working from solid facts? Was timing an issue?

Keep your own score and rate your performance. Stay positive...only those who do things can err. The manner in which one handles mistakes differentiates a successful leader. By analyzing the results of your decisions, you can refine your thought process and, with practice, make better decisions.

Action Items:

Learn form your mistakes—list one situation where you acted on unfounded information and what you could have done to avoid that.

Session 25
Preparing for the Future—Part I

Ready or Not, Here it Comes

…and you have to deal with it. **It's the** *future*!…and being prepared for the future is unquestionably a top priority of managers and is at the heart of leadership.

…but here's the rub I often hear…"I'm running a business—you think I have time for guessing about what may or may not happen? No one can know the future."

O.K., fair enough; but If that's your reaction, I encourage you to rethink your position and stick with me as I list some basic actions for managers and some reasons for identifying and evaluating potential events that could affect your business. To free up some time for you to do that, I'll discuss some actions you can take. Managers must work on both fronts…taking care of today's business and positioning the business for the opportunities and threats of tomorrow. No question, though, that caring for the current cash-flow takes priority, but somehow you must find time to look to the future.

If you routinely operate with a weather eye on the likely "what ifs" and have contingency plans in place, you already know the benefits. Just consider this a reminder to review your process for gathering "best guesses" about the future.

As I write this session, I am also preparing for *"A Business Tune-Up"* interactive workshop at an annual business conference. The concepts mentioned here help form the "framework for thinking" I believe are necessary to run your business. We will work with some of these in the workshop. Next session in Part II, I'll follow-up on comments and discussions from the workshop.

You Can Probably do Anything…just not Everything

The argument about not enough time to do everything is valid. I find it to be the number one issue named by managers. And that proves the point…you must prioritize. During 2003, when American Airlines interviewed me for the in-flight audio business channel, the first question was, "What's bothering your clients? In what area do they seek help first?"
My response then was, "Time—they need guidance in making the most of their time."

Today clients ask a different question; "How can I organize the business and put the infrastructure in place for maximizing the effectiveness of my business?" Actually, same issue merely asked using different words.

You must be able to manage the present before you can expect to shape the future.
So, what's your best approach in handling the dual challenge of running the business today and preparing for tomorrow?

Time Management!

Right! Managing where you spend your time is the only answer. You know that: the difficulty comes in the execution. That's why I've selected the topics I've written about in the preceding sessions. I believe these are important management tools for running a business. Successful managers have demonstrated the effectiveness of these practices over the years. Managing through the proper use of these tools will help you get things done and to instill the confidence in yourself and others that you know how to lead the business to its goals.

It's up to the manager to create the culture of the business unit. You accomplish this through your personal behavior in managing the business.

People should clearly know what you value and what's important to you. I've written about building your business on the "bedrock" of *honor* and the "foundation" of *discipline* and *accountability*; now start the structure with the building blocks of:

- Establishing the policies, systems and procedures

- Providing the direction and resources

- Putting the right people in key jobs

- Providing for the future of the business.

Things to Do

Experience has taught me that successful managers apply the above in five primary areas of responsibility. Review the following to ensure you have developed and implemented the business tools in managing:

- People

- Product

- Plan

- Protection

- Process

Having the infrastructure in place for the people, plan, product and process and using them to manage the business will enable you to allocate time to look to the future as an integral part of protecting your business.

O.K. that's our review of basics. Now, here's the "take-away" from this writing:
You will ensure a higher probability of successfully providing *protection* for your business if you are prepared to act when un-expected events occur. To be prepared you must:

- Consider possible events

- Assess the probability of them happening

- Evaluate potential challenges/opportunities for your business

- Explore actions open to you

Many events that can affect your business are beyond your control...and afield from your area of expertise. How can you stay informed? I'm at my allotted word-count now. Next session I'll address techniques for gathering information for contingency planning.

Action Items:

List where you spent your time today. What percentage was in "Planning, Leading, Managing"? Was it the most effective use of your time? If not, list what you will do differently tomorrow.

Session 26
Preparing for the Future—Part II

Peering into the Future

Last month we addressed the need to have policies, systems and procedures in place and functioning, as a way to carve out more time for you to devote to strategic thinking. I addressed topic in one of my interactive presentations, "The Business Tune-up Workshop", where we focused on maximizing the performance of your business "engine" so the day-to-day operations would require less attention. One of our goals of both of these efforts is to minimize the time spent "fixing" things, allowing more high-value time for preparations to protect and advance the business in the future. All managers spend some of their time "in the future"…and depending on your position and responsibilities, the focus of your business and the immediacy of events that affect your business…deciding *where to spend your time* may be high on your list of management details. How you balance your time between managing the present and preparing for the future is a key management issue…especially in today's environment. So, now that you've arranged this "strategic thinking" time, how will you optimize your efforts?

Let's look at some actions that can help refine your intelligence gathering procedure. These suggestions are for long-term programs…and I realize they may be more "philosophical" than "immediately practical", but they are important management tools that you should not allow to become rusty. The burden falls on you to work with the concepts presented here to develop your own planning processes based on your specific circumstances. I can offer only some guidance as to how you approach it. Consider this topic as a long-range program. Think about the points included here, plant them in your sub-conscious, let it work for you and over time develop your ideas about future changes.

What You Can Control; What You can Influence and What You Cannot

This responsibility to prepare your business for the future can be daunting...and getting your arms around *this* "puzzlement" is a big deal. Set aside some quiet time to think about this and pursue it as you would to learn any skill. Read, listen, analyze and learn form others...and keep at it. To establish a starting point, list all the things you can envision affecting your business and the way in which you do business. Identify short-term events and long-range trends and assess the probability of them being mere "blips" or long-term trends. This is not easy and your success rate at predicting the future will probably be low. However, the probability of your business being prepared for future events will be greater than if you only reacted to events after they happen.

Accept the fact that you'll never get it 100% right, but be confident that by addressing these things, you will have a far greater probability of success (achieving your goals) than leaving it to chance and reaction. Successful management requires discipline, focus and a healthy dose of reality. Keep testing your fundamental premises to confirm their viability; things change and what you could control yesterday may be out of your control tomorrow. Don't allow yourself to be fixated on the daily "roller-coaster" effects. Study diligently to detect trends and take prudent actions to position your business accordingly.

Listen to the Experts...and Beware the Experts

There's no shortage of those ready to give advice (including me through this column) but to whom do you listen? Overcome the tendency to listen only to those who agree with you or support your beliefs. Identify those who present reasonable hypotheses and supporting arguments on both sides of an issue and develop your own path. There may be times when you accept one person's position on a topic but be aware of the risk. The actual outcome of events is usually somewhere between the extremes the experts predict.

Research any topic and you'll find "experts" who arrive at very different opinions from the same "facts"…and most of them sound very convincing, but you know *some* must be wrong. Listen any day to the TV and radio financial reports and to what the analysts predict will happen tomorrow. Do you make investment decisions based on the opinions of only one? If so, how do you decide which one you think will predict correctly? Most investors I know listen to the predictions of the analysts—both the optimists and the pessimists—and make their own decisions. Sure, they make mistakes, but they learn and over time develop a style that makes money over the long run and lets them sleep at night. I suggest that you apply similar practices in preparing for future changes.

What to Watch

The entire foregoing dissertation is pointless until you decide what you will monitor. You cannot watch everything but you can develop a "feel" for key trends. The trick here is to identify **leading indicators** for your business. You're looking for expected changes in the *status quo*. Not an easy task…it takes time to develop the relationships…and to top it off, most likely something will happen that changes the relationship. Therefore, you must continually confirm the influencing factors. Today, events have far-reaching consequences…nothing happens in a vacuum. Look at how events in the Middle East affect the pump price. What will you include in your list? Start with the "obvious" local or industry-specific events and expand to include other local and global events. Break your list into your ability to "control", "influence" and "no control." Those that fall into the "influence" or "no control" categories require that you plan actions you **can** take to minimize the negative influence and to position your business for later opportunities. (Side note: the Chinese symbol for "crisis" is a combination of the symbols for "danger" and "opportunity").

I believe changes in the following will influence most of our businesses; how will they affect yours? You cannot control any of these but they are indicators; what can you do to best prepare? Listen to the forecasters; think about their predictions and get ready to take advantage.

- Demographics of your markets

- Exchange rate of U.S. dollar

- Out-sourcing of services

- Relocation of jobs

- Business practices of major businesses

- Un-employment rate

- Home sales

- Durable goods sales

- Government actions—new laws, reporting requirements, trade tariffs

- Weather

- New technology

- Mergers & acquisitions

- Business failures

- Politics in other countries

Gather information on these and other factors on a schedule that will keep you aware of the trends. Government reports and political/financial analysts are good sources.

Action Items:

List the three indicators that are most important to your business. Monitor them regularly and track the trends. Plot it for emphasis.

Closing

I trust that you have read most, if not all, of the Sessions and completed the actions listed at the end of each; but that does not mean you are finished. Management is an on-going learning experience. Use this book every now and then as a reminder to check on the effectiveness of your management systems and procedures.

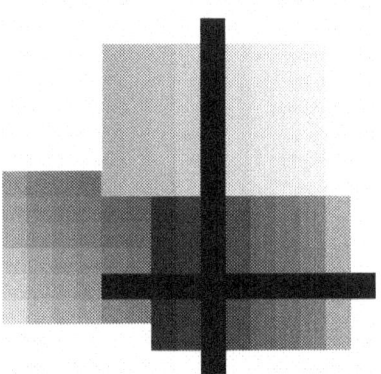

I wish you much success and enjoyment in your adventure.

0-595-31568-2